3 —

Hope
pictures

We
love
you

wish
you

96

love you
Very Much
the beautiful
flowers.

Love,
Chris, Sharon, Jennifer & Mark

JOHN PAUL II
PORTRAIT OF A PONTIFF

BARNES
&NOBLE
BOOKS
NEW YORK

CONTENTS

PHOTOGRAPHS
Gianni Giansanti

TEXT
Marco Tosatti

EDITOR
Valeria Manferto De Fabianis

DESIGN
Patrizia Balocco Lovisetti

TRANSLATION
Jane Glover

© 1996 White Star S.r.l.
Via Candido Sassone, 24
13100 Vercelli, Italia

This edition published by
Barnes & Noble, Inc., by
arrangement with White Star S.r.l.
1996 Barnes & Noble Books

01 00 99 98 97 96   5 4 3 2 1

Library of Congress
Cataloging-in-Publication
Data available

ISBN 0-7607-0161-x
M10987654321

This book was produced with
the help of the press office of the
Holy See.

The photographs have been
produced with the collaboration
of Sygma Agency, Paris, France

1 One of the most celebrated ceremonies: the Palm Sunday celebration in St. Peter's Square.

2-3 John Paul II caught in one of his most characteristic poses: after giving the closing blessing at the end of the ceremony he greets the pilgrims with his arms raised, a gesture which has nothing to do with accepted papal protocol, but one which never fails to delight the crowds.

4-5 Bahía Blanca, Argentina, 1987. Addressing the crowd about Argentina's "Dirty War" and the desaparecidos, the Pope expresses his desire for "profound, fraternal reconciliation, to put an end to hate and to rancor forever."

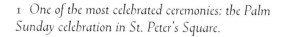

6-7 *A solemn mass is celebrated in the Sistine Chapel. Sixtus IV summoned Michelangelo to start the fresco cycle on the vault in 1508; some years later the artist's Last Judgement concluded the magnificent work.*

8-9 *Krakow, 1983. Poland after the Jaruzelski coup: "I ask you to call these weaknesses, these sins, these vices, these situations, by their names. To fight them without ceasing."*

10-11 *The Hill of Crosses, Lithuania, 1993: "To commemorate the sons and the daughters of your land, those who were tried, those who were imprisoned, sent to concentration camps, deported to Siberia, condemned to death." Although partially destroyed several times, the Hill of Crosses has always been rebuilt.*

12-13 Panama, April 1987. The Pope in a moment
of spiritual isolation during the reading of the Gospel.

13 (top) October 16, 1978. On the day he was elected,
John Paul II spoke with humility: "If I make mistakes
. . . if I make mistakes you will correct me."

INTRODUCTION

eter reigned for twenty-five years. The present Pope, the Courageous Pope, leads the way toward the threshold of the twenty-first century of Christianity — his sights, his thoughts and his desires fixed on the horizon of the next millenium. A weary prophet, like Moses tired by the journey, he leads his people — sometimes a little recalcitrant, sometimes a little distracted by the many temptations — toward the challenge of the third millenium. Since the moment a few years ago when he admitted to being old and began to joke about his health, there have been times when he has seemed to be husbanding his strength, like a traveller who is determined to arrive at his destination, whatever the cost, and knows that he cannot afford to squander his energy. Tired, but determined not to give in. "Before Christ," he said a few months ago, "I renew my vow to serve the Church as long as He wishes, giving myself up completely to His holy will. I leave the decision on how He will free me from this service entirely up to Him."

There is no doubt that the climb has become progressively steeper for Karol Wojtyla. Whereas in the past his strength would allow him to toss children into the air and catch them before handing them back to their proud and astonished parents, now he just pats them, planting a kiss on their heads. His crosier, the outward sign of his power and of his duty, which in the past he grasped strongly and sometimes even wielded, serves more as a support now. A man whose physique bears the signs of a life lived unstintingly, he would have every right to want a little rest. Everyone remembers the almost fatal attempt on his life on May 13, 1981 (John Paul II is convinced that the Virgin Mary miraculously intervened on that occasion). In 1992 he was hospitalized for 16 days at the Gemelli in Rome after undergoing surgery to remove a tumor. The stumble during the audience at the F.A.O. in November 1993 put him into an uncomfortable plaster cast (he broke a small bone in his shoulder) and, lastly, in April 1994, he had a fall in his bathroom, necessitating yet another race to the Gemelli and to the tiny papal suite, consisting of two rooms, which is always in a state of readiness to

receive the Vicar of Christ on Earth, where he had a femoral prosthesis applied to his right leg. He got back on his feet again, with difficulty at first and with a pronounced limp, then gradually regained confidence, but not his previous agility. Skiing, so dear to Pope John Paul II, has vanished from the pontifical agenda.

If we add to this list of misfortunes the constant tremor in his left arm (either the result of the assassination attempt in St. Peter's Square or a symptom of a neuro-muscular complaint) and, according to informants in the papal palaces, a back condition which dates from the Second World War, borne all these years with discretion and courage, there would be every reason to arrange a quieter life. But Pope John Paul II has something altogether different in mind. "We shall have the whole of eternity to rest," he said some years ago, returning from a particularly onerous trip, when someone pointed out that his schedule for the next day was already filled with tiring commitments. This, it seems, is the real key to interpreting the Pope's deepest motives, the thread which embroiders the somewhat incredible story, with its overtones of a twentieth-century fable, of a little boy from deep in provincial Poland who became the most famous personage of this century's closing years. No other Pope in history, and perhaps no other man, has been so photographed and so filmed, nor has any Pope ever held the world's media stage for so long a period and with such dominance. He is a man who has already gone through four epochs and is about to enter a fifth, leading the Church into the third millenium. He knew the rural Poland of the period immediately following the First World War, the Industrial Revolution and the drama of the war with Nazi Germany, the Communist regime, which was expected to last for a thousand years, and then the sudden, dramatic collapse of the Eastern bloc of Communist countries, with its legacy of unsolved problems, smashed hopes, social and human disorder.

Karol Wojtyla was born in Wadowice, a small town in Poland, on May 18, 1920, to Jozef and Emilia Kaczorowscy. His father was a professional

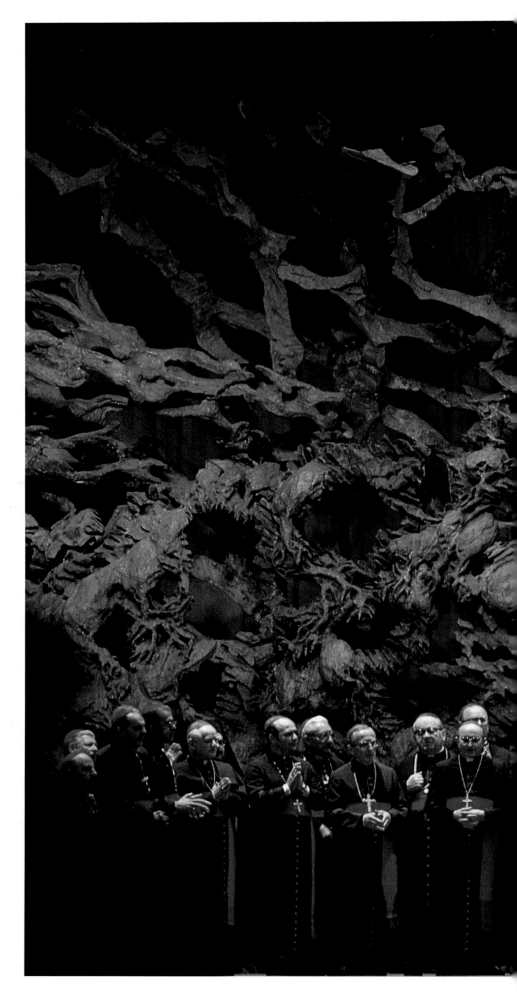

14-15 *General audience in the Nervi Hall.*
The hall is named after the architect who designed it.
A sculpture of Christ by the Italian artist Pericle
Fazzini dominates the background.

16-17 *Another of Pope John Paul II's regular appointments: the Sunday Angelus from the window of his study in St. Peter's Square. The Angelus is usually an opportunity to comment on current events of a particularly interesting or serious nature.*

soldier pensioned off early due to poor health. When "Lolek" was only nine years old, his mother died from a kidney infection. The shadow of premature death was to leave a heavy mark on Lolek's life — a sister had died at a very early age, before he was born, and later, in 1938, a scarlet fever epidemic cost him his elder brother, a doctor at Bielsko Biala on the Czechoslovak border. He moved to Krakow with his father to continue his education, but a year later, on September 1, 1939, Hitler invaded Poland. Five days later Nazi troops entered Krakow, and, in order to avoid deportation or the concentration camps, along with many other young Poles Karol found work on the factory floor, in his case, with the Solvay company. This is how the Pope himself describes his experience, in his book *The Nest I Came From*: "In September 1940 I started work in the Zakrzowek stone quarry. In the summer of 1941 I moved into the factory, working on the water purifying plant for the boiler room. After the accident in 1944 [the Pope was knocked down by a German truck] I was moved to the carbonated division. I left work at the beginning of August 1944 to take up my studies again in the third year of the metropolitan seminary." In the meantime his father had also died, of a heart attack.

These were the crucial years in which the young Krakovian student with a passion for drama, both as actor and author, and for writing poetry (under the pen name of Andrzej Jawien) metamorphosed into the future priest and bishop. These were also the years when, some say, the young Karol was brushed by the scent of an earthly love, of a mysterious woman who appeared in his life before he entered the clandestine seminary in Krakow. His friend and biographer, Mieczyslaw Malinski, dismisses the rumor with a laugh. The story of a young woman who was killed and her lover from Wadowice who decided to turn to the priesthood is indeed a true one; it does not, however, involve Karol Wojtyla but another Polish prelate, Monsignor Kuczkowski.

During his time in the factory Lolek studied and prayed. One of his companions at that time has this to say: "At around midnight during the night shift, he used to kneel down and pray right in the middle of the shop-floor . . . not all the workers there showed respect for his devotion. Some of them used to chuck rags or other things at him, to distract him."

18-19 *Before the assassination attempt it was quite normal to see the Pope's white jeep among the crowds in St. Peter's Square.*

19 (top) *The ejected bullet case lying on the cobbles in the basilica courtyard bears witness to the drama that has just taken place: the attempt on the Pope's life.*

19 (bottom) *Roses that a pilgrim had intended to hand to the Pope are left on the steps next to the empty chair.*

20-21 *Thousands of people praying in St. Peter's Square for the Pope's life on the evening of the assassination attempt.*

22-23 *A general audience in St. Peter's Square: the Pope's hand and the pilgrims' hands.*

24-25 *Two children greet the Pope in Baltimore in October 1995.*

But he had already made his final choice: on November 1, 1946, Karol Wojtyla was ordained into the priesthood by the celebrated Archbishop of Krakow, Cardinal Sapieha.

After the agony of the Nazi madness, the world moved into an era known as the Cold War and dominated by two groupings of states. New and unimagined horizons were opening up to the young boy from Wadowice. It was the start of the *cursus honorum* that would lead him to Rome, first as a theology student at the Domenican Angelicum college, and then into a rapid crescendo of appointments. He taught philosophy at Lublin University and was appointed bishop and then auxiliary at Krakow. He took an active part in the Second Vatican Council, and on January 18, 1964, Pope Paul VI appointed him Archbishop of Krakow.

Karol Wojtyla has been called the world's parish priest. It is an apt title, even though it encapsulates only one of the facets of his personality, and it was in the 1960s that the future Pope laid the foundations of his great pastoral and political activity in Poland. The boys at St. Florian's, Krakow, where he was just a lowly priest, called him "Uncle," and so did the girls at St. Anne's parish, whom he used to take walking in the mountains around Zakopane. His was a direct, uncomplicated relationship with the faithful, accompanied by intense involvement in cultural activities to combat the Communist regime. He founded the Institute for the Family, gave help to a political movement called ZNAK, which adopted a critical stance toward the government, and worked hard to get the theological faculty set up. Those were the years of the celebrated battle of Nova Huta, when the government blocked the attempt to build a new church in this industrial satellite town. The harshest period of the battle would occur when Solidarity, the free trade union founded in 1980, lent its support to the fight. But by that time Wojtyla had already gone to the Vatican in Rome; the battle finally ended in 1989, with the collapse of the Communist regimes in central and eastern Europe.

In 1967 forty-seven-year-old Karol Wojtyla was the youngest cardinal in the Roman Catholic Church, but it was already some years since Lolek had first crossed out of the borders of Krakow and Poland to visit the Polish communities spread around the world, as far away as Papua New Guinea. Travelling is another aspect of the *cursus honorum* and an indispensable part of achieving high office in the church. It is a way of becoming well known, of establishing direct relations with local churches, and of discovering the facts and diverse requirements of particular situations and problems light years away from each other. Pope John Paul II would visit very few countries that Archbishop or Cardinal Wojtyla had not already seen.

The strange tale of the little boy from Wadowice ended — or was it just beginning? — on October 16, 1978, in St. Peter's Square with the words "If I make mistakes . . . if I make mistakes, you will correct me." He was the first Slav Pope in history, the first non-Italian since Hadrian VI of Utrecht was elected in 1522. Since that October day there have been seventeen years of eventful history: the first visit to the Rome synagogue; the friendship with Sandro Pertini, President of Italy; Solidarity and the confrontation with Jaruzelski; the prayer meeting for peace with all the world's religions at Assisi; the "rehabilitation" of Galileo; the collapse of the "Evil Empire"; twelve encyclicals, eight apostolic exhortations, the same number of apostolic "Constitutions," and thirty apostolic letters, as well as a sea of speeches. To date he has called ten Synods and six consistories. He has proclaimed 731 new beatifications and 272 saints. "He is still alive," he jokingly replies to young people who greet him with cries of "Long live the Pope," and on the flight to the United States at the end of 1995 he said, "You can see for yourselves, I am well, the Pope is still alive." He is tired and a little worn, but nevertheless determined to celebrate the great event — the Jubilee that will mark the beginning of the twenty-first century, the dawn of the third millenium of Christianity — in Rome, on Mt. Sinai, and in Jerusalem. But he would also like to go to China, to Cuba, to Moscow, and to Lebanon. His schedule is already filled up for the next few years. For the moment, albeit with a slight limp, he is still on his feet. In the words of a Polish hymn, "Walk on, walk on, Dabrowski, from the land of Italy . . . ."

THE VATICAN,
THE CITY,
THE STATE

26-27 *From the liturgical point of view the beatification ceremony is one of the pontificate's most spectacular moments, particularly when it takes place in Christianity's "head" church. The photograph is of the beatification of Monsignor Escrivà de Balaguer, in May 1992.*

29 *The dome of St. Peter's, seen here from inside the basilica, is Michelangelo's architectural masterpiece. Beneath it, in the true center of Christianity, are St. Peter's tomb and the Altar of the Confession, surmounted by Bernini's canopy.*

The Vatican is first and foremost a tomb; indeed, it is *the* tomb— the tomb of the first Pope and Prince of the Apostles. According to tradition, Peter was crucified there during a particularly ferocious persecution of the early Christians. He chose to be executed upside down as a sign of humility toward Christ, who died with his eyes raised toward heaven. He was buried there, some eighteen feet below the basilica's high altar, the splendid bronze construction created by Bernini. The altar is known as the Altar of the Confession because that is where the old fisherman confessed his faith in Jesus Christ and underwent martyrdom.

Tradition was reinforced by papal authority in 1968, when Paul VI gave official confirmation that one of the burials excavated in the grottoes underneath the basilica was that of the first Pope and had Peter's reliquaries placed in the niche in nineteen Plexiglas containers. So the Vatican was founded upon a burial stone, at the time of the Emperor Constantine, the first basilica being built in honor of Peter — and the other martyrs who shared his fate on the hill — conferring a unique charisma on the most important Roman Catholic basilica in the world. The memory of the Prince of the Apostles is everywhere in the church: "Tu es Petrus . . . thou art Peter and upon this rock I will build my church." The evangelical formula runs in large capital letters along the base of the cornice, above the drum of the apse. In the nave stands the bronze 13th-century statue of St. Peter, so greatly venerated that the right foot is worn from pilgrims' countless kisses and touches. Bernini's *Gloria* in the apse incorporates *St. Peter's Chair*, an extraordinary work decorated with ivory, and a gift of Charles the Bald to Pope John VII.

The Vatican and St. Peter's are the roots, the tangible, physical symbols wrought in stone and marble and bronze, of the Church's spiritual power. They form a mosaic that is steeped in history, tradition, faith, and politics. It is the only complex of its kind in the world, similar to but greater than other sacred sites: the Qabaa at Mecca, the Temple site and West Wall in Jerusalem, the Ganges at Benares. A hill which was surrounded by marshes and fields in Roman times, the *ager vaticanus*, a name of Etruscan origin perhaps, is now probably one of the places with the highest density of works of art and history in the world, as well as a city, a state, and the seat of government of one of the most influential and widespread religions on the planet.

The first walls and towers were built on the hill by Pope Leo IV, round Constantine's basilica, in the 9th century, in part to defend against the Saracen raiders who were bold enough to sail up the Tiber. In the 12th century, Pope Innocent II added an inner ring of walls. In the 13th century, Pope Nicholas III, an Orsini, started building a two-story palace, the kernel of successive extensions and buildings from the Renaissance right up to the present, with St. Peter's as its center, the richest and most grandiose Roman Catholic church in the world. It is not John Paul II's episcopal seat (St. John Lateran is), nor is it his "parish" (this is St. Anne of the Palfreniers, next to Porta Angelica), but it represents the *Sancta Sanctorum* of the Roman Catholic Church. It is here, on the basilica's central balcony, that the new Pope makes his appearance on leaving the conclave by which he has just been elected; he gives most important messages, *urbi et orbi*, to the city and to the world, from the central loggia. On his return from every apostolic journey he goes to pray on St. Peter's tomb, and once a year he hears confession, just like any ordinary priest. The Pope takes his legitimization

30-31 *Writing of Michelangelo, whom he calls "one of the Titans of art," Victor Hugo says that the artist "superimposed the Pantheon on the Parthenon and created St. Peter's." Despite the basilica's colossal size — 430 feet high by 613 feet long — critics stress that the harmony of its proportions restores the monument to a "human" scale.*

32-33 *The culminating moment during the ordination*
of eleven new bishops by the Pope in St. Peter's basilica.

and his power from Peter's tomb: he is the Bishop of Rome, the Vicar of Jesus Christ on Earth, the Successor of the Prince of the Apostles, the *Pontifex Maximus* of the universal Church, the Patriarch of the West, Primate of all Italy, Archbishop and Metropolitan of the Roman Province, Sovereign of the Vatican State and City. "Holy Father" or "Holiness" are the most direct and colloquial names for this man who rules over just 108 acres packed with buildings, more than fifty-five thousand square yards of them. Gardens, twenty or so courtyards, and around one thousand rooms of all sizes contain innumerable quantities of precious art objects, furniture, books, paintings, and manuscripts. Not everything inside the walls has been catalogued or described. This is particularly true of some sections of the Vatican Library, where this work is currently being undertaken. It is because of this incredible density that article 24 of the Lateran Treaty declares the tiny state as neutral in perpetuity and inviolable. Any hostile action, however limited, could produce irreparable damages. The Vatican was spared during Allied bombing raids on Rome during the Second World War, although one night an unidentified aircraft dropped some small-caliber bombs which caused insignificant damage. The mystery has never been cleared up, for although the device had been made in Great Britain, a deliberate provocation could not be ruled out. Since 1954 the entire Vatican has been protected under the Hague Convention, and in 1984 the Vatican City was formally declared part of the World Art Heritage. However, in 1984 a bunker below the Cortile del Belvedere was inaugurated to store the precious codices, manuscripts, and documents belonging to the Library and the Archives.

The border between Italy and the Vatican is invisible. It runs from the end of Via della Conciliazione at St. Peter's Square, where the third arm of Bernini's collonade (had it been built) would have closed in the immense 70,000-square-yard space that can hold 300,000 people. The Vatican State is miniscule, but like an enormous dime store, it houses the most disparate of objects: a functioning railway station and the *Osservatore Romano*; the Post and

Telegraph building and a heliport; the polyglot Vatican Press and the Pharmacy; the Swiss Guards' barracks and arsenal and the Mosaic School. Then there is St. Martha's Hospice, a residential complex for visiting prelates and nuncios; the tapestry restoration workshops and the first headquarters of the Vatican Radio; the Papal Academy of Sciences, gardens, vegetable plots — fresh vegetables for the Pope's table as well as honey from the papal hives — and the Ethiopian College; the Tower of the Winds, Nervi Hall, and the Palace of the Holy Office. This does not include the museums and the papal palaces, the true nerve center of the universal Church.

The Pope is ruler of all this and much more besides, and his rule is absolute. In form at least, he is the last absolute sovereign left in the world, as absolute as the Sun King, Louis XIV, or Philip II of Spain, more so than Elizabeth I of England. The Constitutional Law promulgated on June 7, 1929, and still in force, gives the Pope all legislative, executive, and judicial power. His person unites everything that modern states divide among parliament, government, and the judiciary. He is a sovereign by divine, not elective, right, drawing his power from God Himself. The conclave is only a system to designate him; the electing cardinals do not transfer any of their power to him, they are simply the Holy Spirit's tool.

From the papal palaces the Pope guides and controls three parallel structures. The first, and smallest, of these is the Vatican City, the miniscule relic of temporal power which is guaranteed to the Pontiff so that he can exercise his moral and pastoral power in total freedom, without being influenced by any state. Then there is the Holy See (i.e., the international organ which accredits ambassadors and appoints papal nuncios, and which has differing levels of diplomatic relations with around one hundred and twenty nations throughout the world), the Pope's official and diplomatic face. Finally there is the universal Church, closely linked from an operational standpoint with the Holy See, but not automatically identifiable with it. It is a complex arrangement where many of the possible problems and demarcation conflicts are resolved due to their common

34-35 The washing of the feet is one of the most significant of the Easter ceremonies. Here John Paul II is seen taking part in the ritual in the basilica of St. John Lateran.

36-37 St. Peter's Square provides the visitor with the greatest of all Baroque scenarios. The immense court covers 70,000 square yards, one-sixth of the total area of the Vatican. It is indeed the foreground to St. Peter's basilica, the ideal stage for the Church's great liturgies.

38-39 *The Secret Archives, built and decorated in the 17th century on orders of Paul V, store documents of great historic and artistic importance.*

dependence on the Pope's absolute authority.

The Church's first task is to defend and to spread the Roman Catholic doctrine, and the Vatican has, over the years, supplied itself with the necessary tools. Thus there is a Congregation for the Doctrine of the Faith (previously the Holy Office), whose function is to ensure that bishops, theologians, and priests do not express any opinions contradicting the consolidated doctrine of the faith and to punish those who do. There are over four thousand bishops in the Roman Catholic Church, and a Congregation is needed to oversee their nominations, transfers, and everything else concerning this sensitive sector. The Congregation for the Clerics has the same function with respect to priests, while the role of the Congregation for Monastics is to supervise the many Sacred Orders; these orders are in fact allowed considerable autonomy (which they guard jealously), the only exception being the Jesuits, who are bound to the Pope by a vow of total obedience: *perinde ac cadaver*. The very powerful Congregation for the Propagation of the Faith (its prefect is known as the Red Pope, while the General of the Company of Jesus is called the Black Pope) keeps a watch over the missionary churches, especially in Africa. At the head of it all is the Secretariat of State, which flanks the Pope — in the physical sense too, as the offices are in the apostolic palaces. This is the Holy See's political organ. It has a Secretary of State (currently Cardinal Angelo Sodano), whose position could be compared to that of a head of government. One section of the Secretariat acts as a Ministry of Foreign Affairs and is divided into linguistic sections. It plays a very important role in the general life of the Church, particularly in the preparation of the Pope's trips and the writing of his speeches. The Pope makes dozens, if not hundreds, of speeches each year, but very few of them are written personally. The Secretary of State also coordinates the work of the nuncios, the Pope's ambassadors, throughout the world.

Around twenty-three hundred people work in the Vatican: thirteen hundred lay people, including around three hundred women, and eight hundred priests or members of religious orders. In the past few decades the Curia, including the College of Cardinals,

40-41 *The restoration of the Sistine Chapel, which was paid for by a Japanese company, brought back the original colors of Michelangelo's masterpiece. In the photograph, Gianluigi Colalucci examines the Romanie Cumaean Sybil prior to its restoration.*

has experienced an accelerated rate of internationalization, and the reign of the Slav Pope has naturally accentuated this trend. Very few of these employees live within the walls, and there are only a small number — not counting the diplomats — who carry a passport issued by the Holy See.

Life inside the Vatican City is bustling in the morning, when the coming and going through Porta S. Anna (St. Anne's Gate) is quite intense. The Swiss Guards and the Vatican's security service have their work cut out keeping watch over the "border" crossing. In the afternoon the city seems to slip little by little into a torpor, until the moment late in the evening when only the Swiss remain to guard the gate. A reminder of times long passed, they are the only picturesque element remaining from earlier times and other Pontiffs. It was Julius II, the terrible Della Rovere Pope, who recruited the first Swiss in 1505 for use in the Italian wars. The Swiss Guards are all that remain of the many pontifical guards (including a little-known Corsican Guard in the 17th century) down the centuries. Famous for their loyalty — in 1527 they sacrificed themselves in combat with the Constable of Bourbon's Lansquenets, in order that Clement VII might escape to Castel Sant-Angelo by the Borgo Passetto — they are all volunteers. Signing on for two-year contracts, the majority are recruited from the German-speaking Swiss cantons, and they live, for two years at least, in the barracks at the Porta S. Anna entrance. Wearing their blue-and-orange-striped uniforms, with puffed sleeves and big hats, or breastplates and morions, armed with halberd and sword, they are the delight of camera-wielding tourists.

Everything about this state is different, especially as far as its finances are concerned. Is the Church poor? It seems incredible, but it is to some extent true, and the Holy See, the central office of Roman Catholicism, is particularly in need. The Vatican City, i.e., the physical part of the state, has its own budget and makes a profit thanks to the museums. The Holy See, or rather the ministries, the Secretariat, the Vatican Radio, and *Osservatore Romano*, in addition to the nunciatures around the world, cost around 158 million dollars annually.

The only income is from the rents collected on real estate, the yield from the "dowry" bestowed by the Italian state in 1929, and the offertories from the dioceses all over the world to cover the costs of central government. The biggest contributors are the U.S. bishops, followed by the Germans, and for some years now, the Italians, thanks perhaps to a miniscule levy on income tax. The payroll is the largest item of expenditure (around 67 million dollars). The Vatican Library and Press cost around 18 million, but they produce a small profit. The Vatican Radio and *Osservatore Romano*, on the other hand, produce no

dividends other than the spiritual kind and cost around 4 million dollars and 19 million dollars respectively. The "Voice of the Pope" broadcasts regularly in forty different languages, including Arabic, Chinese, Aramaic, and Swahili.

42-43 *The Swiss Guards, pictured here on sentry duty at the Bell Arch (one of the entrances to the Vatican next to St. Peter's), are one of the more fascinating aspects of Vatican folklore. A large part of their charm is due to the blue-and-orange-striped uniform, perhaps designed by Michelangelo, and their Renaissance swords and halberds.*

44 The Swiss Guards' barracks are opposite the Church of St. Anne of the Palfreniers, adjacent to St. Anne's Gate, the busiest entrance to the city-state.

45 *The Guards are all recruited according to the terms of a special treaty between Switzerland and the Holy See. Here one wears a morion, a Spanish-type helmet of the Renaissance period, with a large plume.*

46-47 *The Vatican treasures include many tapestries, some of which are extremely valuable. This type of work is subject to deterioration over time, so the Vatican has a specialized workshop, operated by nuns, for this kind of restoration.*

47 *The Osservatore Romano, the Holy See's unofficial daily newspaper, was founded in 1861. It comes out every afternoon except Sunday and carries all the official news about the Holy See, in addition to comments and opinions on important current events. It is also published in English, French, Spanish, German, Portuguese, and Polish, although not daily.*

48-49 *This unusual picture is of the stairway at the entrance to the Vatican Museums. Every year millions of people from around the world come here to admire the works of art in the galleries. The 1994 visitors' total was 2,690,091.*

50-51 *The Gentlemen of His Holiness welcome important visitors in the San Damaso courtyard. Since 1964, when Paul VI announced to the nobility that the papacy no longer had the financial means to maintain traditional functions and services, the Gentlemen in black tailcoats — the untitled now outnumber the aristocracy in their corps — have replaced the Pope's privy chamberlains, who used to wear a black, Renaissance-style uniform.*

51 *A group of cardinals leaves Nervi Hall at the conclusion of a session of the Synod. (A synod is a congress where representatives of the universal Church, or of one particular church, meet to discuss practical matters such as training for the priesthood, religious life, and the place of the laity within the Church.)*

52 One of the most solemn events in the Church's calendar is the opening of the Holy Door. Normally bricked up, it is opened once every twenty-five years in celebration of Jubilees.

53 The Pope, immediately after entering the basilica through the Holy Door, at the start of the extraordinary Jubilee in 1983.

54 *The Pope seated beneath Bernini's canopy at the Altar of the Confession. Bernini drew the inspiration for his twisted columns from an Egyptian column long held inside the basilica.*

55 *John Paul II enthroned during a solemn ceremony in the true heart of Christianity, that part of the Vatican basilica constructed over St. Peter's tomb. Behind him is the St. Helena, the best-known work of Andrea Bolgi, a pupil of Bernini.*

56 Faith feeds upon symbols and images. The gold cardinal's cross is the symbol of the "Princes of the Church," men chosen to constitute the Senate of Catholicity and the potential electorate of Popes. Red, a "noble" color in many cultures, is especially significant in Roman Catholic symbology since bishops and cardinals must witness to the faith usque ad sanguinem — as far as martyrdom.

56-57 *John Paul II places the cardinal's berretta on the head of the Bishop of Sarajevo, Monsignor Vinko Puljic, in November 1994.*

58-59 *A photograph of His Holiness during the Family Synod in 1994 catches him in a tired moment, but the arrival of a child with a candle for the Pope is all that is necessary to revive him.*

60-61 *A cross in the center of the Coliseum in Rome commemorates the Christians martyred there. One of the most evocative ceremonies of the Easter period in Rome, the Via Crucis, or Stations of the Cross, is led by the Pope across the ancient stones of the Flavian amphitheater.*

62-63 *John Paul II has never missed the Via Crucis in the Coliseum. At Easter 1995, despite his obvious difficulty in walking after a hip operation, he insisted on completing the stations and even holding, briefly, the heavy cross at the head of the procession.*

PRIVATE LIFE

64-65 *The Pontiff signing a document in the Library. This is the room where John Paul II, like Paul VI before him, has met and talked with the powerful of the earth: Gorbachev, Reagan, Clinton, and Yeltsin have all sat at this table.*

66-67 *Every morning John Paul II spends time in silent meditation in the private chapel, while a nun prepares the altar for morning mass.*

68-69 *John Paul II at prayer in his private chapel, while in the background guests wait to take part in the morning celebration of mass.*

*S*olitude is the burden of every Pope and especially of the current incumbent. It is a solitude packed with people, busy with engagements and crowds, but this does not make it any lighter, or any less continuous or threatening. The solitude of a Pope is that of a man burdened with an enormous responsibility, a weight that caused Paul VI to suffer and that crushed John Paul I. It is the solitude of a helmsman steering a ship that is not his own — the Church — in a world like "the dark night of the soul" that Karol Wojtyla's favorite mystic, Giovanni Della Croce, writes about. "The Pope is the most solitary man in the world" has been a truism in the Vatican for decades. But John Paul II fills this definition with his own particular style. His is the solitude of a mystic, of a man continually searching for the final Being. His is a special kind of solitude, closely connected to his way of praying and of working. When he was Archbishop of Krakow, writes Mieczyslaw Malinski in *My Old Friend Karol*, the first biography of Wojtyla as Pope, "he used to pray in that characteristic stance of his, leaning forward, his head resting on one hand, the palm covering his face, or with his head resting on both hands. He used to stay in the same position for long periods at a time." And like many solitary travellers of the road which leads to the absolute, his prayer took extreme forms: "He would sometimes lie prostrate in the shape of the cross" on the floor in front of the altar. "His driver told me, after he had entered the chapel by mistake once."

In Krakow, Wojtyla would write, read, and pray in the chapel. In the Vatican the chapel is his first commitment every day. The Pope rises, not very willingly, at around 5:30 a.m. Apparently he has never liked early starts. Paul VI had some exercise equipment installed in the private apartments and John Paul II has continued to use it, adding some specific rehabilitation apparatus — a harsh necessity after his accidents. Then he goes to chapel to pray and meditate. The chapel, which was refurbished under Paul VI, is not very big. There are two bronze doors by Enrico Manfrini, illustrating episodes from the life of Christ. A single column holds the most simple of

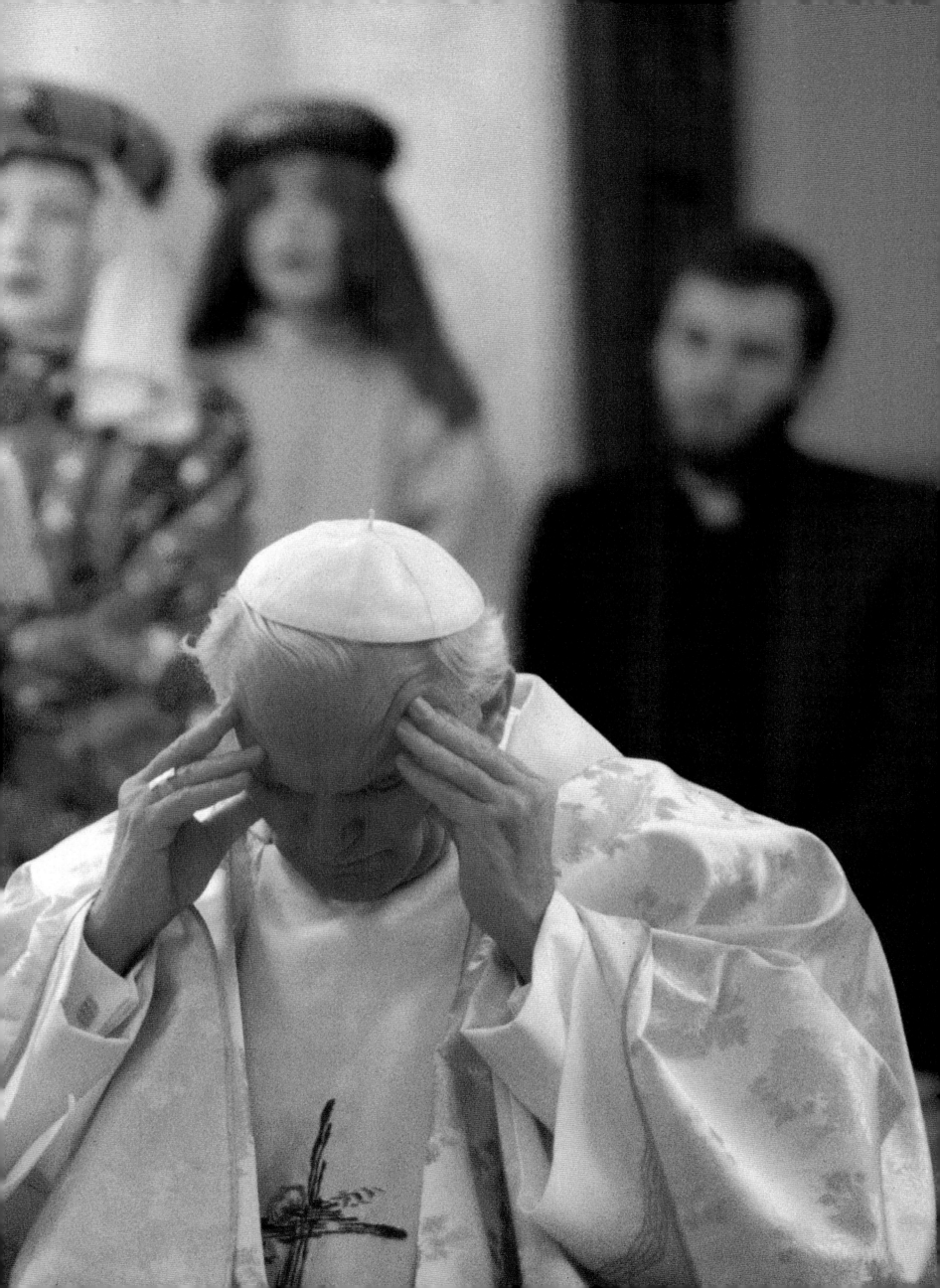

altars in white marble. In the background is the
martyrdom of Saints Peter and Paul. The bright,
stained-glass ceiling is the work of Luigi Filocamo.
A host of angels surrounds the risen Christ in glory.
At exactly seven o'clock, John Paul II celebrates mass.
Every day the nuns of the Sisters of the Sacred Heart
Order of Krakow, who look after the Pope's
housekeeping and cooking, and his private secretary
Monsignor Stanislaw Dziwisz, a discreet and attentive
figure who has been in the Pope's service since
Krakow, attend this mass. Sometimes there are

guests. A few days beforehand, each of the fortunate
invitees receives a telephone call from Monsignor
Stanislaw: "This is the Pope's private secretary. Would
you please be at the Bronze Gate at 5:30 a.m.?"
The Pope celebrates mass slowly, in Latin, Italian,
or Polish, but the language chosen for the liturgy may
depend upon the nationality of the guests, a
particularly courteous gesture. It is always an intense
celebration; the Pope allows a long time for the
prayers of preparation and the giving of thanks after
the Eucharist. At the end he greets his guests in the
nearby Library, saying a few words to each of them
while the official photographer takes the ritual snaps.

Breakfast comes after mass, either with guests
or just people from the household. The table is a
simple rectangle, with ten chairs at the most, all
identical, with the same high backs and arms.

70   When mass is over, John Paul II greets a group of Korean guests in the nearby Library.

70-71   In the Library once more, the Pope has a few words with his guests.

72-73   Breakfast is a valuable time to start the day's work. The Pope talks with Cardinal Stephen Kim about the program for a visit to Korea. Seated on his right, his private secretary Stanislaw Dziwisz and, on his left, his secretary at the time, Emery Kabongo.

74-75 *The Pope goes back into the papal residence,
accompanied by Monsignor Jacques Martin. The
Raphael Loggia, so-called because it was decorated
by the painter from Urbino, is on three floors and
looks out over the San Damaso courtyard, opposite
a wing of the Pope's private residence.*

There is only one difference in seating: the Pope sits alone on one of the long sides of the table, with no one next to him. The menu is very simple: milk, coffee, cheese, jam. The bread, which is already on the table, is the Roman "rosette" that Karol Wojtyla has loved since he was a young priest. "I came to Rome especially to eat these bread rolls with no center," he said to a fellow student who offered him a slice of wholemeal bread, "and you're offering me the ordinary stuff." Breakfast lasts no longer than half an hour, after which John Paul II works until eleven o'clock, reading documents, studying reports, and writing. He still does this by hand but will soon have a computer. The chapel is in front of his private study and he visits it frequently, to help him concentrate and to find inspiration — and help — in the choices and decisions he has to make.

Afterwards, the Pontiff leaves "home" to begin the official part of his day. It is a modest house, all things considered: the papal apartments take up the last two floors of the east wing of the palace built by Sixtus V. The dining room, bedroom, and study are comfortable but very sober. There is no longer the opulence of the red damask, which Paul VI had removed. Pastel colors predominate, with dark furniture of simple design. Some of the floors, which Paul VI preferred in wood, are now covered with pale tiles. It is easy to pick out the papal apartment from St. Peter's Square. The last window on the far corner of the palace, on the last floor, is the bedroom; the second window lights the private study (the one from which the Sunday Angelus is pronounced); and the next two central ones give onto the drawing room. The chapel is opposite the study, on the inside of the palace, while the dining room faces in the direction of the Tiber, toward Via della Conciliazione and the Passetto di Borgo. The overwhelming impression is one of great simplicity, a little disappointing, perhaps, for the admirers of the 17th-century Baroque of the Church of Rome. Paul VI swept away the last vestiges of the court, consigning to history the "noble ecclesiastical antechamber" and "His Holiness's majordomo," all the "ecclesiastical servants," the "secret valets," the "common chaplains" (one person alone looks after Pope John Paul II: Angelo Gugel,

77 For the first time ever, and to the amazement of those pilgrims present, one Good Friday the Pope entered St. Peter's and began to hear confession like an ordinary priest. Since then the "Pope's confession" has been repeated every year as part of the Easter ceremonies.

who has been in the Vatican a lifetime), as well as the three army corps (dissolved in 1970), including the Noble Guard of the Sword and Cape and the Palatine Guard. The pontifical household is now run by one man, with the title of Prefect: Monsignor Dino Monduzzi. He is responsible for looking after many aspects of the Pope's public life, including the weekly Wednesday audiences in St. Peter's Square or in the Nervi Hall, which regularly attract thousands of pilgrims and tourists. A typical year for the Pontiff involves around five hundred audiences in addition to the general Wednesday ones. The term "audience" is a vague one, covering everything from a visit by a head of state to a meeting with representatives from one of the professions.

As eleven o'clock draws near, the Pope leaves his second-floor apartment and goes to the private Library, a large room used by the Popes who were "imprisoned" in the Vatican by the *bersaglieri* at Porta Pia during the Italian war of unification, and by their successors this century. The main piece of furniture, and the most famous, is a desk in the monastic style, which has been silent witness to historic talks and surprising encounters. The Empress Zita, widow of the last Austrian monarch, Charles I, came to the Vatican and was welcomed by Karol Wojtyla with the words, "It is my pleasure to greet my father's sovereign," a reference to his father's service in Galicia, now part of Poland but once part of the Austro-Hungarian empire. The Library is the true throne room for this solitary monarch, solitary even in his secret pain. A foreign prelate tells the story of how in 1985 he would go every day to teach the Pontiff the rudiments of his language in preparation for one of the Pope's trips abroad, so that he could surprise the pilgrims who came to hear him. As the Pope stood up during the lesson he was unable to hide a grimace of severe pain. "Holiness, you are in pain," said the prelate. "Never repeat that," replied the Pope, his voice suddenly serious.

History, in the form of its great protagonists, has walked the Library's checkered tiles in the seventeen years of this pontificate. A crowd of heads-of-state, ambassadors, bishops visiting *ad limina apostolorum* (after each five-year period in office, every bishop has to travel to Rome, back to the "threshold," the tomb of the apostles Saints Peter and Paul, to give an account of the situation in his diocese), nuncios, politicians, the heads of religious orders, and the Pope's "ministers." The Pope follows the news daily on television and in the newspapers, but the audiences, especially with the diocesan bishops, are his eyes and ears on the world — a direct contact which often does not end in the Library. "There are two things you never know with the Holy Father," says one Monsignor jokingly. "What time he will eat and how many people he will invite to eat with him." The Pontiff's predecessors ate alone, or in very restricted company. John Paul II has transformed lunch into an instrument of government and of work. The last audience in his schedule will sometimes continue at the table, with guests from widely varying fields: specialists in a particular field if he is preparing an encyclical or other document, members of his own staff, nuncios, bishops, or just friends, such as Professor Styczen, Wojtyla's pupil in Lublin and his successor to the chair of moral theology, and Dr. Wanda Poltawska, a psychiatrist and expert in "natural" family planning methods and the Pope's consultant on women's affairs. Her friendship with John Paul II is an old one, and she may have been the receiver of one of Padre Pio's miracles. In 1962 she was waiting to be operated on for cancer. Wojtyla, a bishop at the time, asked the friar who bore the stigmata to pray for her recovery, and the tumor disappeared mysteriously.

In the afternoon John Paul II rests a little, then takes a walk, usually on the large terrace of the papal palaces, where he reads the breviary and meditates. Halfway through the afternoon he goes

78-79 One of John Paul's typical expressions as he listens to a member of his team. According to his friend and biographer, Mieczyslaw Malinski, the Pope "has developed an enormous ability to concentrate."

80-81 During a break from work, in the privacy of his bedroom, John Paul II allows his gaze to wander over the roofs of the capital.

back to work, meets the closest members of his staff, and draws up documents. After dinner, the rosary and the recital of the *compieta* end the Pope's official day, but not his study. He is a fervent, omnivorous reader: St. Augustine, Martin Buber, Walt Whitman, St. Thomas Aquinas, Dostoevsky, Rilke, Mircea Eliade, Levinas, Wittgenstein, and Cyprian Norwid. He will read at any time, even during journeys. Monsignor Dziwisz always has room in his bag for whatever book the Pope is reading.

Sometimes the Pope takes time off to enjoy himself. If he is at Castelgandolfo, he swims in the modest pool (59 feet by 26 feet) that the Polish community in the United States gave him, or spends time with friends. In 1988 he organized a dinner in the Vatican for twenty ex-pupils from the Wadowice high school, his final-year classmates. There had been forty-two of them; twenty were dead, ten having died during the Second World War. Jerzy Kluger, a Jewish friend of the Pope's who lives in Rome, led them through the Bronze Gate to a party where the main dish was pizza — the real, Neapolitan pizza — even though it had been made by the Polish nuns, who alternate Mediterranean dishes with typical central European ones. It was an emotional and nostalgic occasion, and so, they say, is Christmas. Mainly Polish in style, except for the presence of the crib, the dinner is *maigre*, without meat. There is always carp, prepared in gelatine or with a sweet grey sauce containing sultanas, and there is always a cheesecake of which the Pope is particularly fond, along with poppy-seed cake. Pius X's biographers say that he would be seized by homesickness for Venice whenever he heard a train whistle, even in the distance. Pius XI would talk about his excursions in his beloved Lombardy mountains. Pius XII, John XXIII, Paul VI, and John Paul I were surrounded by brothers, sisters, nieces, and nephews, constituting a family (sometimes rather in the way). John Paul II has only a distant female cousin to whom he is not very close, and so at Christmas he breaks the *Oplatek* — a rectangular host bearing scenes of the Holy Family — at a table with his secretaries, the five Polish nuns, and Angelo Gugel. Solitude is indeed the Pope's seal, but there are times when this Pope seems more alone than the others.

82-83 *John Paul II reads through some documents during a walk in the Vatican gardens. At the beginning of his pontificate the Pope liked to walk in the gardens, but he later abandoned the custom when it became inconvenient.*

83 *During the very early part of his reign the Pontiff lived in the John XXIII tower in the Vatican gardens while his private rooms were being prepared.*

84 *Deep in thought, the Pope puts his signature to a document. During his pontificate he has published twelve encyclicals, eight apostolic exhortations, and thirty apostolic letters. Each bears the Pope's arms on the cover — the triple crown, the keys, and his crest, consisting of a cross and the letter "M" for Maria, engraved on a shield — and the holograph signature of John Paul II in Latin.*

85 *The Pontiff during a speech delivered live on television from the Library. Perugino's Resurrection can be seen in the background.*

86-87 *The Pope praying in the Hall of Investiture, where once the cardinal elected to the throne of Peter by the conclave received his new vestments.*

88-89 *A late stroller in St. Peter's Square will often see a light shining in the Pope's private study.*

89 *John Paul II ends his day with prayer in the private chapel before retiring. When he is in the Vatican, John Paul II spends a good deal of time thinking and praying in the chapel.*

PAPAL JOURNEYS

90-91 Seoul, South Korea, 1984. "Your ancestors embraced such overwhelming spiritual realities, like Confucianism and Buddhism, that they truly made them their own, delving deep within them, living them."

92-93 A special area is prepared for the Pope on long flights. Here he is reading the Breviary during a journey to Argentina.

94-95 U.S.A., 1995. The Pope leaves the aircraft that has taken him from New York to Baltimore.

W hy does the Pope — this Pope — travel so much? This is the immediate question which springs to mind. Everyone, in fact, can see how different the present pontificate is, not so much from Paul VI's reign, but from the tradition of priestly immobility of Popes in recent centuries. Pope John Paul II's reply is a very short one, but one which has infinite implications: "The problem of the universal Church is to make it visible."

The universal Church: if it were not such an irreverent idea one could think of it as a multinational company with a soul and for the soul, the most widespread multinational on the planet, with branches in every continent and in every country, and a great number of problems. Never, in its two-thousand-year history, has the Roman Catholic Church been so big and had such internal diversity. Think, for example, of the yawning diversity in culture, customs, way of life, and sense of what is sacred between a parish in Frankfurt, Germany, and one in M'Bwanza, Congo; between the church in New Guinea and the patriarchate of Babylon of the Chaldees. It is Rome itself, the faith and the doctrine, which acts as the great adhesive force in this mosaic, and in people's eyes it is the Pope who supplies the visible sign of this unity. He is a concrete, tangible instrument, not just a metaphorical one. During a journey to Lima the security service had to restrain two girls who in their enthusiasm wanted to scratch the Pope to get a piece of his skin, as a holy souvenir.

It is a multinational whose branches — the local churches — are constantly increasing, becoming more powerful and more protective of their own autonomy. It is in close competition with many other bodies, *ad maiorem Dei gloriam*, to provide salvation: Islam, wealthy and expanding in Africa; sects and new religious movements in South America; the traditional culture of Eastern Asia, a wall from which the Church, after centuries of effort, has managed only a few chips of conversion; and not forgetting what the Pope himself considers to be the most

96-97 *La Paz, Bolivia, 1988. "Drug consumption has become the trading of freedom, it has become the worst kind of slavery, of corruption, of death. The drug trade is, from every point of view, an abomination."*

98-99 *Guadalcanal, Solomon Islands, 1984. John Paul II was welcomed by Prime Minister Mamaloni and took the salute from a very British-style honor guard.*

100-101 *"La Serena," Chile, April 1987. John Paul II intended this journey to be one of hope for national reconciliation in a country torn by political strife.*

insidious rival of all: materialism, the permissive society that reduces everything, including men and women, to consumer items.

So the Pope travels, in order to parade Rome in every corner of the world, in every church, no matter how out of the way or how insignificant. This is the message: Rome is, it exists and it is still, as in the times of Peter, for the Roman Catholic faith at least, *caput mundi*. Everywhere the Pope goes, he puts on the scales something that no other religion can offer: God's Vicar on Earth, a figure of tremendously powerful sacred charisma that inspires awe in the masses. Even now, despite the fact that advancing age and infirmity have to some extent dulled his edge as an orator, he can still move tens, even hundreds of thousands of the faithful — and it is difficult for anyone who has not witnessed it to understand — to paroxysms of enthusiasm with a single word, a gesture, or a sentence.

"One must travel to live and live to travel," John Paul II is reported to have confided to a friend once. When questioned about the truth of this anecdote by his biographer, Frossard, he replied, "I don't remember, but I can't deny it, either." The apostles travelled too, is the comment from the Vatican, and the Pope does not hesitate to defend this characteristic of his pontificate. "I know too that there are some people who do not approve of these journeys," he said, on his return from Latin America in 1985, "and this fact is what confirms my belief that they must be made." Whatever the cost. To anyone who asked him, at the end of an exhausting two-week tour in 1986 — taking in Bangladesh, Singapore, Fiji, New Zealand, Australia, and the Seychelles — if the results were worth so much effort and such a high cost (paid by the local churches), he replied, "Yes, yes, it's worth it, it's worth it; I believe that we cannot count the cost when we are bought at an inestimable price. Do you understand? There is no cost for this. It is stupid to talk about cost and to try and stop the Pope. The cost. He costs more than the Queen! Thank God, because the message he brings has a transcendent value; he brings things which are of great worth and importance." The Queen in question was Elizabeth

II of England. Her visit to Australia shortly before
the Pope's had cost much less.

John Paul II visited the Chilean dictator,
Pinochet, in the Casa Rosada and the Sandinista
regime in Managua, where he faced a violent
demonstration during mass. He shook hands with
Jaruzelski in June 1983, six months after the anti-
Solidarity coup, and he met Alfred Stroessner, the
pro-Nazi ruler of Paraguay. The list of dictators and
presidents of pseudo-democratic Third-World
regimes greeted on the tarmacs of innumerable
airports is a long one. The Pope has visited Angola
and Mozambique, countries torn apart by civil wars,
when the ceasefire was fragile and the guns still
warm. He experienced the *apagon* — total electrical
blackout — in Lima, caused by the Sendero
Luminoso, and widespread hostile demonstrations
in Holland, Switzerland, Austria, Federal Germany,
and the United States, not to mention the storm
over Maseru in Lesotho, which led to a damaged
plane and a forced landing in Johannesburg when
the apartheid regime was still in power — the
reason for discounting a possible visit in the first
place. "I cannot avoid risks. I have to meet the
people, the rulers and the politicians," the Pope has
explained. "Perhaps sometimes politics is a sinful
thing, and perhaps there are sometimes sinful
rulers. But one cannot ignore this political
dimension of life, especially in the life of a nation.
When I went to Africa for the first time, I was
delighted to see states which had been under
colonial powers until a few years earlier finally
enjoying their own sovereignty. Perhaps it was an
imperfect sovereignty, not yet translated into
democratic principles, but at least those people
were the bosses in their own homes."

"You can cut off my hands if Wojtyla
manages to stay more than two consecutive weeks
in the Vatican," was the spontaneous comment of
his friend Jerzy Turowicz, on Wojtyla's election,
and the prophecy has proved true. A reverse
Copernican revolution, begun by Paul VI, has
become a characteristic feature of the pontificate.
Rome no longer waits, passively, for the local
churches to come to her, she moves out toward the
edges. Four international journeys and eight in Italy

102-103 *Calcutta, India, 1986. During his visit, the Pope went to the house which the priests of the goddess Kali gave Mother Teresa to look after the dying homeless: "Oh most tender and compassionate God, bless all those who are dying, all those who are soon to meet Thee face to face."*

every year have become the norm. *El trotamundo de la paz* is what one South American newspaper called him (other, equally vivid headlines read, *el Maradona de la fe* and *el goleador de la Iglesia*). He has now more than covered the distance to the moon and back and has set off on a third crossing.

The Pope's journeys, with his staff and a small number of accompanying journalists, have become a separate category of events, with their own rules and protocol. Some are written, others are not, but this does not make them any less binding. John Paul II's first flight from Rome was in January 1979, just three months after his election,

his destination the Dominican Republic, Mexico, and the Bahamas. Alitalia prepared a bed for him, as it does on all intercontinental flights, a real bed in the front of the cabin, using Paul VI's sheets. Despite his age and his troublesome health, Montini had been no mean traveller; the sheets were silk, and John Paul II let it be known that he preferred cotton ones. "He wants a humbler style," said his entourage, but the Holy Father dismissed the suggestion, saying simply that silk sheets stuck to his body.

The Pope always leaves Rome with Alitalia and usually returns by the national airline of the last country on his tour. He is accompanied by a considerable number of his "top-level management": the Secretary of State and the Substitute Secretary of State, as well as the Prefect of the Papal Household and the indispensable presence of the Papal Master

104 Morocco, 1985. An historic kiss: John Paul II is
welcomed at Casablanca airport by the "Head of the
Believers," King Hassan II of Morocco, who invited
him to address young Muslims in the city stadium.

104-105 Casablanca, Morocco, 1985. The only mass
meeting between the Pope and followers of Islam:
"Christians and Muslims must bear witness to Him,
in word and deed, in a world which is increasingly
secularized and sometimes even atheist."

of Ceremonies, Monsignor Marini, who assists him at all religious functions. Then there is the head of the Vatican Radio and of the *Osservatore Romano* (the Vatican newspaper); the Pope's doctor, Professor Renato Buzzonetti; his private secretary, Monsignor Dziwisz; his valet, Angelo Gugel; and Father Tucci, who, since 1982, when he replaced Monsignor Marcinkus, has been in charge of organizing the papal trips. The entourage is, of course, accompanied by members of the Vatican security service and the Swiss Guard, who change out of their multicolored costumes into sober suits

for the occasion. Lastly, there are the variables: prelates of the congregations closely involved in the ceremonies lined up for that particular trip, cardinals, and members of the episcopal conferences of the countries to be visited.

For John Paul II the hours in the air are almost a holiday, the last restful period before the furious onslaught of meetings, speeches, and travelling that is the daily bread of every pastoral visit. Since the incident in April 1994, the organizers have been wielding the axe vigorously, paring down the papal appointment book, but the days the Globetrotter Pope spends in his travels are packed with engagements and hard work. The front of the Alitalia cabin is converted into a small sitting room with a table crowned by a splendid flower arrangement in white and yellow, the papal colors, or, on occasion, the red and white of the Polish flag.

106-107 *Casablanca, Morocco, 1985. The sovereign of Morocco invited his illustrious guest to his palace for a private conversation before accompanying him to a meeting with participants in the Pan-Arab games.*

108-109 *Sion, Switzerland, 1984. A difficult trip:*
women, theologians, and priests all reproached the Pope
for the Church of Rome's closed attitude.

A crucifix is hung on the wall opposite the Pope's chair, together with an icon of the Madonna of Fatima, an object of his particular devotion: on May 13, 1982, he laid the blood-stained sash he was wearing on the day of the assassination attempt at the feet of the original statue.

Pope John Paul II reads, prays, recites the rosary and — on the outward leg of long journeys, he talks to the press. Yes, the press. Fifty — and the number hardly ever varies — photographers and journalists from the printed press, television, and radio are allowed on the papal flight. Only those who are permanently accredited by the Vatican can even hope to be included on the list. This is the only occasion that journalists can have direct, face-to-face access to the Pope, after which down comes the curtain of privacy, which in recent years has been an increasingly hermetic one. About half an hour after take-off, the Pope appears on the cabin threshold which marks the border between the area reserved for the press and the "forbidden" zone where the entourage is lodged, and answers three or four questions. Familiarity tends to banish awe, and nowadays no one is surprised if the Vicar of God on Earth talks to the press. It was not always so. When Paul VI made an appearance on one of his first trips, the press corps was shaken by a storm of emotion. Many fell to their knees and some were so overcome that they were unable to utter a word. In those days there was an unwritten rule that the Pope could not be questioned directly; he alone could speak. Montini would walk through the rows of seats, stopping to say a few words and hand out the commemorative medals of the trip, and move on.

Even when travelling, the Pope eats and sleeps in his own home: he never accepts the hospitality of the host government. He usually lodges in the residence of the papal nuncio, sometimes in the bishop's palace or with a religious order. The same philosophy dictates that he never participate in official luncheons or dinners. Every one of the trips he has made until now has had its own unique physiognomy, but, obviously, some were more significant than others. The key to interpreting the enigma of this Pope is to be found

in his journeys rather than his Vatican-based activity. They bring him face to face with real political, social, and human situations without the mediation and shield provided by his Roman court, and at the same time they provide an open window onto his own thoughts and feelings. "I . . . could . . . not . . . not go" was his comment on his first trip to Poland in 1979. Since then he has returned to his homeland once every four years, and each visit brings with it intense emotions. In May last year, for instance, he was unable to hide his feelings upon arriving at Bielsko Biala, the small town where his brother died when he himself was still a boy. There have been terrible disappointments too. The Pope's three Polish journeys trace the parabola of his pontificate. In 1979, only a few months after he had been elected to the Throne of Peter, John Paul II crossed Warsaw in a military vehicle painted white for the occasion. It was a triumph. The streets were carpeted with flowers and more flowers rained down from the windows lining the route. When the Pope entered the cathedral next to Wyszynski, the elderly cardinal was deeply affected, and tears could be seen, or rather intuited, on the Pope's face as he wiped his cheek with the back of his hand. The message he took with him was this: "It is impossible to

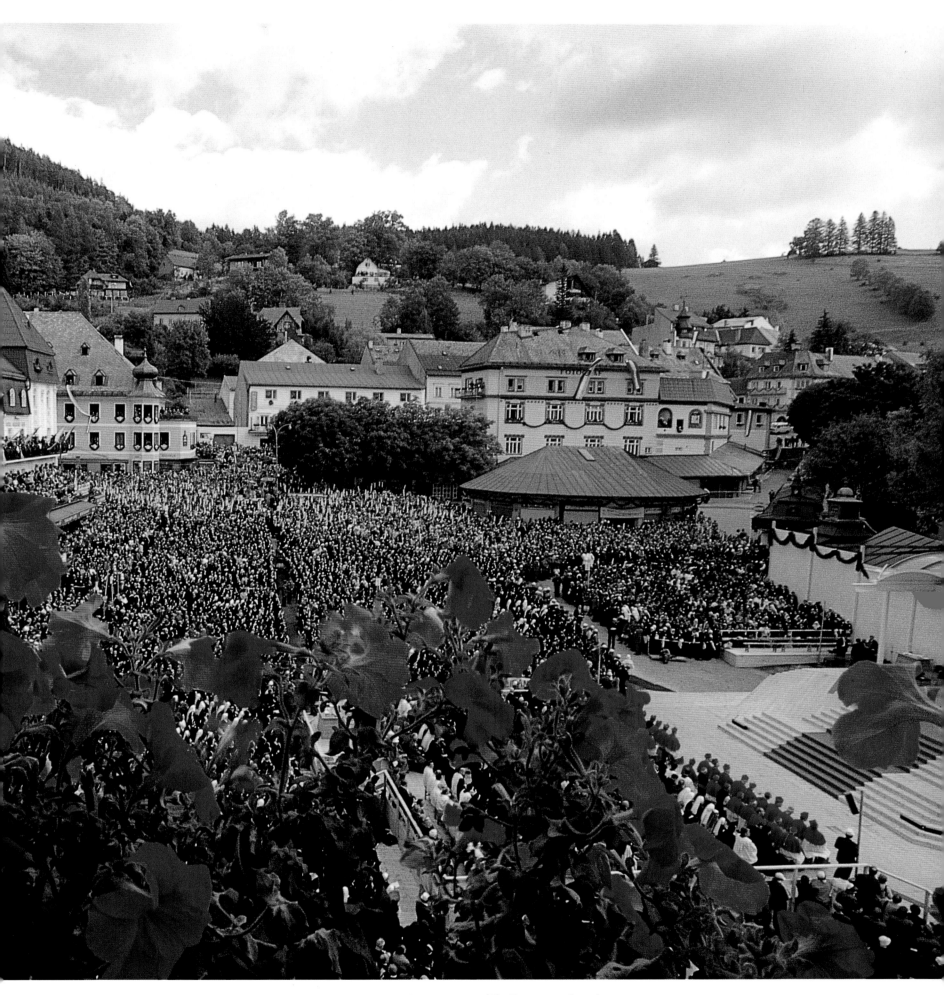

110-111 *Austria, 1983. The Pope remembers the victory of John III of Poland against the Turks, at Vienna. "That victory of Polish troops saved Europe's civilization and Christianity."*

112-113 *Thailand, May 1984. John Paul visits
the refugee camp at Phanat Nikhom.*

113 *Thailand, May 1984. John Paul II visits the
86-year-old monk Vasana Tara, the country's supreme
Buddhist patriarch, at his residence.*

understand this nation, with its splendid and at the same time terribly difficult history, without Christ."

Four years later the scenario had changed. The Solidarity trade union had been outlawed, and the country was under martial law, controlled by the police and the army. It was a penitential journey; even the weather was grey. Huge crowds gathered in a climate of irrational, almost millenarian, expectancy, as if the Pope could turn the situation on its head by magic. There were a million — at least — at Czestochowa, two million at Krakow, where he beatified two nineteenth-century heroes of the movement against the Tsar. "For Kalinowski and Chmielowski," he said, "insurrection was a stage in their journey toward sainthood. They were driven by a heroic love for their homeland. The sacrifice of their own lives for that of their friends manifested itself in their participation in the insurrection." The Church acted as an umbrella for the Poles during the years of Jaruzelski's rule.

In 1991 the Pope went back to a homeland which had been liberated from the Marxist regime. Nineteen eighty-nine had come and gone: the Wall had come down, and what Reagan had dubbed the "Evil Empire" had collapsed. But this 20th-century Moses, after leading his people to victory, found

them gathered around the Golden Calf of abundance and of permissiveness. "We must conquer the works of the flesh, and they are not only fornication, impurity, and libertinage, but enmity, discord, divisions, envy, and drunkenness." Every day he cast aside the official speeches and cried his indignation aloud, improvising *ex abundantia coris* — because his heart was overflowing: "Good behavior is required! Freedom needs maturity. Liberty cannot only be a pretense; that would put mankind into chains — and we must not confuse immorality with freedom. I say this because this land is my mother, this land is the mother of my brothers and of my sisters, and you must all understand that your approach to these things is irresponsible and that these things hurt me and they should hurt you too."

Poland had changed. In 1983 an entire park was not enough when the Pope celebrated mass, but by 1991 the main square in the Old Town was more than sufficient. According to one of the Pope's closest advisers, who wishes to remain anonymous, in order to understand the Wojtyla of today, that journey and that brutal realization must be taken into account; it seems after all that the battle against Communism was a relatively simple one. Today's adversary is more insidious and more powerful. Freed from the fear of favoring the pro-Marxist wings of the Church, John Paul II can launch his most difficult crusade: the challenge of the final years of the millenium against the "virus of rampant materialism, of indifference to ethical values and the consumer society," as he admonished in his lightning trip to Prague in April 1990, celebrating "his" victory amid the still-smoking ruins of one of the most anti-clerical governments in the Warsaw Pact. The elderly Pope has taken up his crosier and launched a new crusade to bring Christianity back to the Western Europeans. The direction Peter's ship will be taking in the coming years of the pontificate has been decided.

114-115 *Honduras, March 1983. The papal procession, headed by the "Popemobile," takes a wrong turn and ends up driving through the dusty streets of a small village.*

PAPUA
NEW GUINEA

116 *John Paul II has visited Papua New Guinea twice, in 1984 and 1994. At Port Moresby he was presented with the typical flowered garland of welcome.*

116-117 *Mount Hagen, Papua New Guinea, 1994. John Paul II was welcomed by a group of dancers wearing the traditional costume.*

118-119 *Papua New Guinea. During the Pope's second trip, in 1994, the fear of attack by Islamic groups followed the Pope even to this remote corner of the planet.*

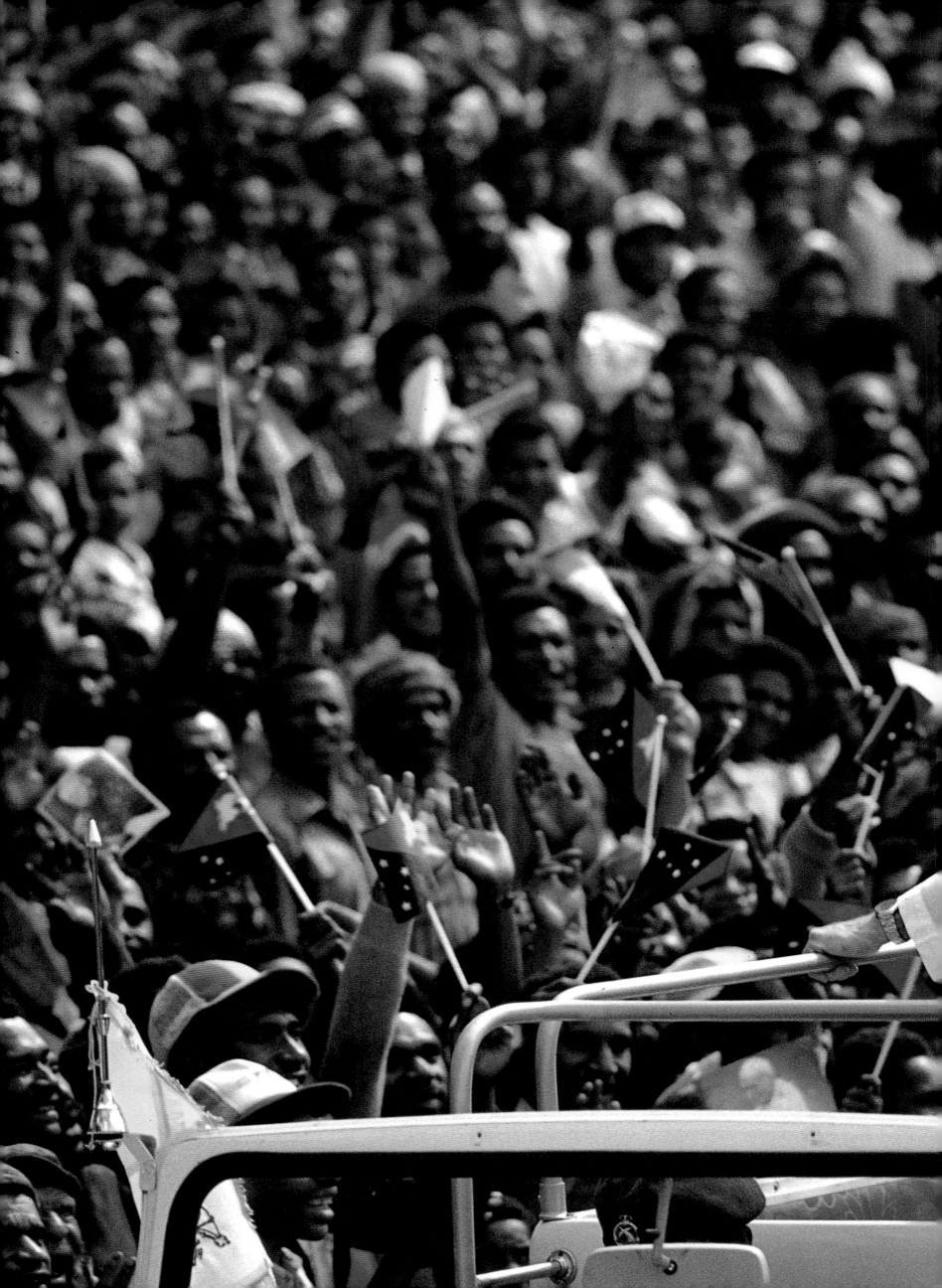

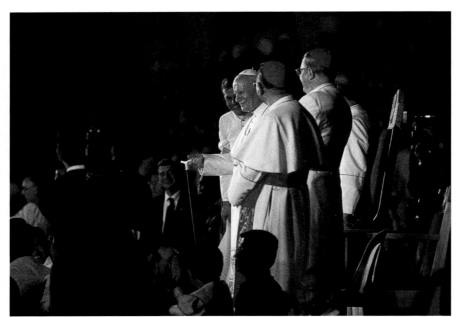

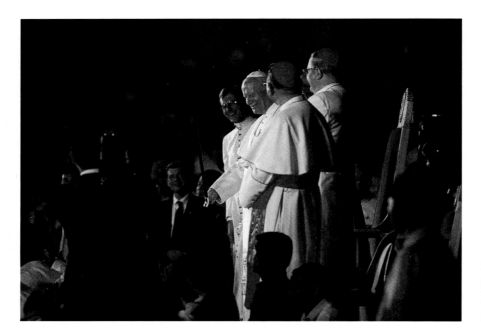

120-121 *Manila, 1995. John Paul II was not yet able to walk properly after his accident on April 29, 1994. Here he plays with his silver-topped cane, rolling it along the stage at his meeting with young people.*

122-123 *Manila, 1995. A huge crowd, three or perhaps four million people, attended the mass celebrated by the Pope. He closed the World Youth Day with these words: "Millions of young people are falling into covert, but real, forms of moral slavery."*

LITHUANIA

124-125 *Mass in Lithuania, 1993. After the election victory over the former Communists, the Pope delivered this warning: "It is very important that those who have lost remember that it is not enough simply to adjust to changed social conditions; it requires sincere conversion and, if necessary, expiation."*

126-127 *Vilnius, 1993. The Pope is momentarily overcome by emotion: "I also pray for all those who have no cross on their graves."*

PORTUGAL

128-129 *Lisbon, 1982. A measureless crowd*
welcomed Karol Wojtyla at Fatima, where he gave
thanks to the Madonna for saving his life from the
assassin's bullet the previous year.

SOUTH KOREA

130-131 *Seoul, 1984. John Paul II's visit was immensely important for Korean Roman Catholics. The Pope prayed for the country's unification in front of a crowd of one million people: "May your beloved country, which has been tragically divided into two parts for more than a generation, be reunited as one family."*

132-133 *Seoul, 1984. "Rapid industrialization and economic development must give birth to a more humane society, with true justice and peace, where all life is considered sacrosanct." Thousands of transparent veils create a kaleidoscope of color as the light shines through them.*

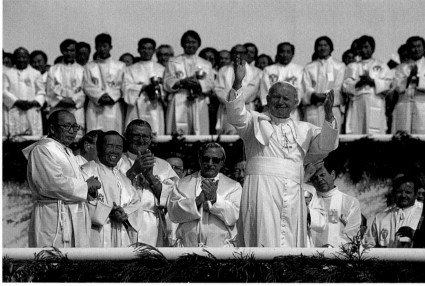

134-135 *Seoul, 1984. Special security measures were implemented to deal with student demonstrations against the government. The courtyard of the seminary where the Pope stayed was filled with clouds of tear gas.*

135 *Seoul, 1984. The Pope meets clergy and monks at the Jesuit university of Sogang.*

FRANCE

136 *August 1983, the Pope at Lourdes. He celebrated mass near the Grotto, before an audience of two hundred thousand pilgrims on the field and the hill opposite the sanctuary.*

137 *Lourdes, 1983. The Pope prays in the Grotto: "I have become a pilgrim and my day here with you will be a simple one, just like any other pilgrim's."*

138-139 *Lourdes, 1983. To young people: "We love the Church too. How we should love it to be more transparent, freer from all kinds of compromise!"*

SPAIN

140-141 *Avila, 1982*. One of the Pope's most triumphant journeys in Europe, during which he admitted that "times like those of the Inquisition produced tensions, errors, and excesses."

142-143 *Guadalupe, 1982*. Christians "must let their voices be heard while at the same time respecting the beliefs of others, in accordance with the values in which they believe."

144-145 *In May 1982, during the Falklands War,
the Pope visited the United Kingdom. Here the
"Popemobile" travels through the streets of London.*

145 (top) *London, 1982. The papal procession moves past Big Ben. This was the first time that a Pope had stepped onto English soil since the Anglican schism. For the first time the Pope was welcomed as a spiritual leader and not a head of state: without gun salutes, national anthems, or military honor guards.*

145 (bottom) *Liverpool, 1982. John Paul II's visit to the United Kingdom during the war with Argentina was greeted with increasing warmth the farther north he went.*

146 *San Salvador, March 1983. Armed soldiers escorted the Pope wherever he went. Bishop Rivera y Damas welcomed him with these words: "The horror of an absurd tragedy is hanging over our people. Holy Father, Christ suffers here in our brothers."*

147 *San Salvador, 1983. The Pope prays on the grave of Monsignor Oscar Romero, killed by right-wing extremists while he celebrated mass.*

GERMANY

148 *Mainz, 1980. Pope John Paul II in prayer at the grave of Bishop Kettler, an advocate for the social rights of workers and immigrants.*

149 *Cologne, 1980. John Paul II visited Germany for the first time since being elected Pope. After a service in the splendid cathedral at Cologne, he met university staff and students and spoke about science and faith, admitting the mistakes made at the time of Galileo: "The Church remembers this with regret; today we are aware of the mistakes and the shortcomings of such procedures."*

150-151 *Fulda, 1980. "Ecumenism is an urgent task" — the words of John Paul II in the land of Martin Luther.*

152-153 *Mainz, 1980. During an important ecumenical conference, John Paul II recognized reciprocal responsibilities at the time of the Reformation: "We all need conversion, we want to recognize that we have made mistakes."*

NICARAGUA

154 Managua, March 1983. Welcoming crowds greet the Pope on his arrival in Nicaragua.

154-155 Managua, March 1983. The Pope addresses a crowd in front of a portrait of Sandino. This was the first time that John Paul II faced a hostile demonstration during mass. His condemnation of the pro-regime "populist church" was greeted with shouts and whistles from the regime's supporters in the crowd.

BRAZIL

156-157 *Bahia San Salvador, Brazil, 1980. John Paul II visits the favelas. "Land is a gift from God, to all human beings."*

158 Rio de Janeiro, July 1980. Numerous pilgrims attend John Paul II's mass at the sanctuary of the Aparecida.

158-159 Rio de Janeiro, 1980. The Pope returns to the nunciature after addressing a gathering of almost two million people. "It was the biggest crowd ever in Brazil," according to the headlines in the press.

ZAIRE

160-161 *Kinshasa, Zaire, May 1980. John Paul II celebrating the centenary of the first Roman Catholic church in the country. A huge crowd awaited the Pope, who spoke of the "scourge of racism."*

ITALY

162-163 *Assisi, city of peace, November 1986. Representatives of all the world's main religions accepted the Pope's invitation to meet in Assisi for a joint day of prayer.*

163 (top) *The Pope climbs up toward the basilica of St. Francis at Assisi.*

163 (bottom) *The Pope at prayer during the meeting at Assisi.*

164 Venice, June 1985. John Paul II in a gondola on
the Grand Canal.

165 Nuoro, October 1985. A moment of rest, or
meditation, during a meeting with townspeople.

POLAND

166-167 *Gdansk, 1987. The Pope went back to Poland in 1987 and visited Gdansk (it had not been possible in 1983). He praised the free trade union, Solidarity: "This word has been pronounced in a new way and a new context here, and the world cannot forget it."*

167 (top) *Tarnow, 1987. The "Pope's Divisions": Polish priests follow the celebration of mass.*

167 (bottom) *Katowice, 1983. Mass is celebrated under torrential rain. The Pope defends trade union freedom before a huge crowd. "No one confers this right, it is an innate right."*

CANADA

168 (top) *Yellow Knife, September 1984. A gift for the Pope: a richly decorated and embroidered Huron jacket.*

168 (bottom) *Toronto, September 1984. Preparations for the Pope's mass. "Attempts to substitute something else for God are all in vain. Nothing can fill the vacuum which He leaves."*

168-169 *Yellow Knife, September 1984. Pope John Paul II in a tepee belonging to Huron Indians. "History provides clear proof that over the centuries your people have been the repeated victims of injustice from new arrivals."*

UNITED STATES OF AMERICA

170-171 *U.N., New York, October 5, 1995.*
John Paul II addresses the General Assembly of the
United Nations at its headquarters. He urged the U.N.
to write a "Declaration of the Rights of Nations,"
so that "we may realize that the tears of this century
have watered the ground in preparation for a new
spring for the spirit."

172-173 *Baltimore, U.S.A., October 1995.*
At the end of his trip, John Paul II appealed to the
United States to "defend the right to life, from its
conception to its natural end, to look after and defend
the unborn and all those who might otherwise be seen
by others as a nuisance or undesirable."

174-175 *New York, U.S.A., October 1995.*
The high spot of the Pope's New York trip was the great
mass in Central Park. In the heart of the city symbolizing
wealth, the Pope said: "You are called upon to 'see to'
the needs of the poor, the hungry, the homeless, and all
those who are alone or ill: those suffering from AIDS,
for example."

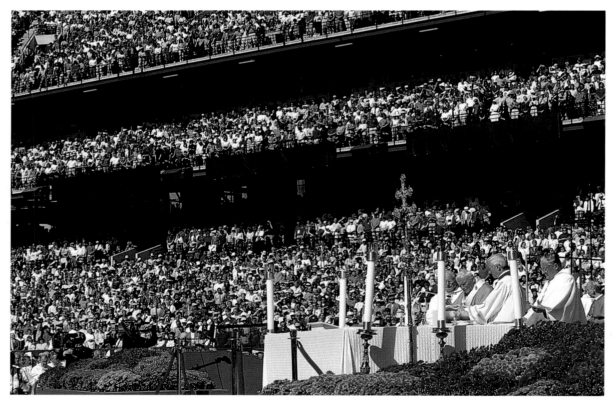

176 *Santiago, Chile, 1987. The Pope hugs a child*
before celebrating mass. "The Church makes common
cause with those of you it sees suffer hunger, cold, and
abandonment."

The author and the photographer would like to thank the following people whose
assistance made this book possible:

at the Vatican:
H.E. Monsignor Patrick Foley, H. E. Monsignor Pier Franco Pastore, Monsignor Piero
Marini, Doctor Joaquin Navarro-Valls, Marjorie Weeke, Vik Van Brantegem, Elisabeth
Fouquet, Suor Giovanna Gentili, Camillo Cibin, Raul Bonarelli, Angelo Gugel, Arturo
Mari, Padre Roberto Tucci, Alberto Gasbarri;

at Sygma:
Hubert Henrotte, Eliane Laffont, Jean-Pierre Pappis, Marie-Christine Ravet, Dominique
Oleon, Valérie Theveniaud, Lionel Cixous, Hélène Mason, Catherine Hertel, Alain
Mingam, Christine Girard, Claude Trentin, François Darmigny, Hélène Legendre, Carole
Couillard;

and elsewhere:
Luciano Mellace, Rudi Frey, Giancarlo Giuliani, Hillary Raskin.

A very special thank you to Anna, Andrea, Greta, and H.E. Monsignor Stanislaw Dziwisz.